Lance Armstrong

Champion for Life!

by Ian Young

Reading Consultant:
Timothy Rasinski, Ph.D.
Professor of Reading Education
Kent State University

Content Consultant:
Sean Petty
Chief of Staff
USA Cycling

Red Brick™ Learning

Published by Red Brick™ Learning
7825 Telegraph Road, Bloomington, Minnesota 55438
http://www.redbricklearning.com

Library of Congress Cataloging-in-Publication Data
Young, Ian, 1970–
    Lance Armstrong: champion for life! / by Ian Young; reading
    consultant, Timothy Rasinski.
        p. cm.—(High five reading)
    Includes bibliographical references and index.
    ISBN 0-7368-3850-3 (soft cover)—ISBN 0-7368-3878-3 (hard cover)
        1. Armstrong, Lance—Juvenile literature. 2. Cyclists—United
States—Biography—Juvenile literature. I. Rasinski, Timothy V. II.
Title. III. Series.
GV1051.A47Y68 2004
796.6'2'092—dc22

                                    2004003560

Created by Kent Publishing Services, Inc.
Executive Editor: Robbie Butler
Designed by Signature Design Group, Inc.
Edited by Jerry Ruff, Managing Editor, Red Brick™ Learning
Red Brick™ Learning Editorial Director: Mary Lindeen

Photo Credits:
Cover, Gero Breloer, EPA Photos; page 4, AFP/Corbis; pages 7, 9, Bud Symes,
Getty Images; page 8, courtesy of Jim Hoyt; pages 13, 45, Joe Patronite; page
14, Tim Scheffer/AP WideWorld; page 17, Pascal Rondeau, Allsport/Getty
Images; pages 19, 36, Mike Powell, Getty Images; page 21, AP WideWorld;
page 23, Corbis; pages 26, 31, DPPI/Icon; page 28, Howard Sochurek,
Corbis; page 33, Harry Cabluck, AP WideWorld; page 39, Joe Raedle,
Newsmakers/Getty Images; page 41, Jana Birchum, Getty Images; page 43,
Jeff Christensen, Reuters Photo Archive; page 48, Mondelo, EFE Photos;
page 51, Jacky Naegelen, Reuters Photo Archive; page 55, PR Newswire
Photo Service; page 59, SportsChrome

Printed in the United States of America.

2 3 4 5 6 09 08 07 06 05

Table of Contents

— Chapter **1** —

A Special Talent

We all have a special talent. What do you do best? Are you good at playing sports, solving math problems, or drawing? As a boy, Lance Armstrong discovered his talent was bike racing. He could ride faster and farther than anyone else. Where might this talent take him in life?

Lance Armstrong and his mother, Linda

Born to Bike

Lance Armstrong was 16 when he tried to enter a senior bike race in Texas. The race organizers thought he was too young, though. They wanted him to ride in the junior race with racers his own age. But Lance had great confidence. He wanted to show everyone how fast he was.

Finally, the organizers gave in. They let Lance race with the seniors. Lance proved he wasn't just confident—he was good. He won the race. Lance is right when he says, "I was born to race bikes."

---

senior: for athletes over the age of 21
junior: for athletes under the age of 21
confidence: the belief that things will happen in a way you want; the belief in your own ability

Young Athlete

Lance Armstrong was born on September 18, 1971. His mom, Linda, raised Lance as a single parent. Linda was both strong and determined. It seems she passed these traits on to Lance at an early age.

In the fifth grade, Lance entered a school running race. The night before the race, he told his mom, "I'm going to be a champ." He was right. He won.

Later, Lance joined his local swimming club. He started cycling the 20-mile (32.2-kilometer) round-trip to the pool every morning. Some days he swam 10,000 meters (6.2 miles). Soon, he was winning swim races as well.

When Lance was 13, he entered an event called the *IronKids© Triathlon*. This was a junior triathlon race that combined swimming, cycling, and running. Once again, he won.

---

trait: a quality or characteristic that makes one person or thing different from another

Special Ability

When Lance was 16, a sports science clinic tested how his body used oxygen. They found Lance could take in and use oxygen more efficiently and effectively than an average person. This meant that his body could perform better during the stress of difficult exercise, such as a bike race.

Lance competes in a triathlon at age 17.

---

oxygen: the gas we need to breathe and live
efficiently: making something happen with the least waste of time, effort, or materials
effectively: working very well

Fast Thrills

As a teenager, Lance regularly won triathlons and bike races. He often beat older athletes. The prize money he won helped pay for his training and bike equipment. It also helped him pay for a new kind of thrill—fast cars.

During his senior year at Plano East High School, Lance rode for a bike team funded by a local bike shop owner named Jim Hoyt. Hoyt paid Lance $500 a month to ride on the team. Hoyt also helped Lance buy a sports car.

Jim Hoyt (right) poses with Lance (middle) and another member of Jim's team.

fund: to give money or materials as a way to support someone or something

A Lesson Learned

Lance won often as a cyclist, but he was arrogant and cocky. During one race, Lance and another rider jostled to get in the best position to win. After they crossed the finish line, they got into a fight.

Hoyt was furious with Lance. He thought Lance should be more mature. To teach him a lesson, Hoyt took Lance's car away. Lance learned a hard lesson that day.

Lance began his cycling career by first competing in triathlons.

arrogant: having too much pride
cocky: sure of oneself in a rude and bold way
jostle: to shove or push roughly
mature: developed fully; emotionally grown

Riding for His Country

Lance was picked for the U.S. National Junior Cycling Team during his senior year in high school. He went to Russia for the Junior World Championships. Lance didn't win, but he learned how to be a better racer. He also met many people who could help him start a career in cycling. The Russian coach said Lance was the best young cyclist he had seen in years.

career: something a person does to make a living; an occupation or profession

School First

All of the training and racing hurt Lance at school, however. He missed six weeks of school, and his grades were low. The school administrators told Lance that he would not graduate from Plano East High School.

Lance's mom wanted him to graduate before starting a sports career, however. She called many different schools in Texas to find a place for Lance.

Lance's cycling success impressed the administrators at Bending Oaks High School. The school would accept him if he would take some courses over again. Now Lance could finish high school and race bikes at the same time!

---

administrator: a person who directs the work of something such as a school or business
graduate: to finish a course of study in a school

The U.S. National Cycling Team

Lance was still an amateur cyclist, but he knew that he wanted to become a professional (pro). He also knew that the best cyclists raced in Europe. If Lance wanted to compete with the best, he needed to leave the United States and race in Europe. But how was he going to do that?

Lance's chance came in 1990, when he was chosen to join the U.S. National Cycling Team. The coach was a former professional cyclist named Chris Carmichael. Carmichael believed Lance had the talent to race professionally one day.

---

amateur: a person who plays sports for pleasure rather than for money
professional: a person who is paid to play a sport

Full-Time Cyclist

Carmichael also knew Lance needed to know more about race tactics. Lance needed more racing experience as well. Carmichael wanted Lance and the U.S. team to go to Europe for a full season of racing.

Carmichael wanted to show the team how hard the life of a full-time cyclist can be. In Europe, the team would experience long hours and tiring travel. They would have to race nearly every day. Lance was only 18, but he felt ready for the challenge. Was he? He was about to find out.

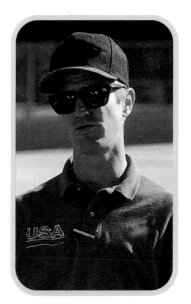

Coach Chris Carmichael invited Lance to join the U.S. National Cycling Team when Lance was only a teenager.

---

tactic: a plan or method used to achieve a goal

CHAPTER 2

The Young Professional

The best cyclists race in Europe. The races are tough, and the racing season lasts nearly 10 months. New riders have to prove themselves in order to gain the respect of other cyclists. Would Lance be up to the challenge? What personal traits would he need to succeed?

Lance rides as a professional in Europe.

Making His Mark

Lance started well for the U.S. National Cycling Team. In 1991, he took the lead in an important race in Italy. The fans wanted an Italian rider to win, though, not this unknown American boy. They threw glass and nails on the road. They wanted Lance to blow a tire, causing him to lose time.

But Lance rode so well that by the finish, the crowd was cheering for him. He won the race, and also the respect of the fans.

Lance's ride also impressed Jim Ochowicz (AWK-oh-vits), team manager for a professional cycling team. Ochowicz asked Lance if he would be interested in racing for his team. Lance was interested, but he also wanted to compete in the 1992 Olympics. Only amateurs were allowed to compete.

Lance decided to remain an amateur. He raced in the Olympics, then afterward, agreed to a contract with Ochowicz's team. At last, he would race as a professional!

---

contract: an agreement that is supported by the law

First Professional Race

In 1992, Lance competed in his first professional race. It was in Spain. The weather was awful. More than 50 riders quit before the finish. Lance struggled at the back of the field, tired and wet. He finished in last place. He thought about quitting and going home to the United States.

But Lance was not a quitter. Two days later he raced again in Switzerland. Lance rode well. In fact, he finished second! Lance's strength and determination impressed the other riders. They began to ask, "Who is this new American rider?"

---

field: a group of athletes

Amateur and Professional

In the past, amateur athletes competed for the love of a sport. They usually did not earn money for competing. Professional athletes were paid to compete.

Today, the differences between amateur and professional are not always clear, however. Many amateurs train and compete full-time. They may also receive money and equipment from sponsors.

Many serious cyclists turn professional at some point. They do this for many reasons. Firstly, the most important races are only open to professional teams. Secondly, many professionals receive contracts. The money they receive from these contracts helps the athletes support themselves and their families.

sponsor: a person who agrees to pay expenses or give other support to another person or group

Racing for a Million

In the early 1990s, interest in bike racing was strong in the United States. One reason was Greg LeMond. He was the first American to win the famous Tour de France bike race. However, LeMond was about to retire. Bike fans needed a new American star to get their interest again. Could Lance become that new star?

In 1993, a U.S. company that owned a chain of drug stores offered a challenge. The company would give $1 million to any racer who won the top three U.S. race events in one year. The company felt certain that this could not be done. Each of the three races required different racing skills. The company did not believe that one racer had all the skills needed to win all three races. Lance traveled back to the United States with one thing on his mind—victory.

Lance won the first two events. These were a road race in Pittsburgh, Pennsylvania, and a six-day race throughout West Virginia.

The final event would be the U.S. Professional Championships in Philadelphia, Pennsylvania. If Lance won that race, the prize was his!

Lance had a reputation as a rider who raced without thinking. He would ride too hard and waste his energy early in a race. But for this final event, he changed tactics.

Lance started the race more slowly. He saved his strength for the last 20 miles (32.2 kilometers). Then he attacked. He raced harder and faster than any other cyclist. Lance won by a record margin. The $1 million prize was his.

Lance felt that he was able to win all three races because of the support he got from his team. To show his thanks, Lance split the $1 million with them.

---

reputation: what people think about a person
margin: the distance between two things

A Great Year

Also in 1993, Lance entered the grueling Tour de France. He was only 21. Most riders don't attempt this race until they are 24 or 25. Younger cyclists simply are not strong enough yet.

Lance began well. He even won a stage. At 21, he was the youngest man to ever win a stage. But a few days later, Lance quit the Tour de France. The race had moved into the mountains, and Lance found racing there to be "too long and too cold."

But the year still ended well. Lance won the Professional World Championships in Oslo, Norway. He was the youngest person ever to win this championship. Lance pumped his arms in excitement as he crossed the finish line.

Everyone wanted to congratulate the youngest-ever World Champion. But Lance was only looking for one person—his mom. "We did it! We did it!" he told her.

---

grueling: very difficult and tough
stage: one part of a race

Tour

A race held over several days or weeks is called a *stage race* or *tour*. Each day, a new timed stage begins. Each stage is usually different. Riders might race over a flat course for one stage and in the mountains for another. Some stages are individual time trials, where cyclists race against the clock with no teammates. The rider who completes all the stages in the shortest overall time is the winner.

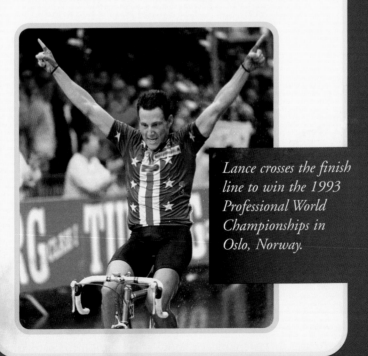

Lance crosses the finish line to win the 1993 Professional World Championships in Oslo, Norway.

A Tour Tragedy

In the 1995 Tour de France, Lance's Italian teammate Fabio Casartelli (FAH-bee-oh CASS-ahr-TELL-ee) was riding down a hill at 55 miles (89 kilometers) per hour. Fabio's bike hit a concrete block and he was killed.

The team was devastated, but they decided to continue racing in Fabio's honor. A few days later, Lance won a stage. He dedicated the win to Fabio. "Fabio was with me," Lance said at the finish.

Crashes are common in the Tour de France. But it is rare for a rider to be killed. Fabio was just the third rider to die since the race began in 1903.

---

devastate: to make helpless; to overwhelm
honor: respect given to recognize a person or a great deed
dedicate: to say thanks or show appreciation for someone

All for One

Cycling is really a team sport. In a race, one team rider will have the best chance to win. So his teammates work to help him. They shield their top rider from strong winds. They carry drinks and food for him. They race ahead to see what other teams are doing. They may even give up their bikes for him, if necessary! These selfless teammates are called *domestiques* (doh-mess-TEEKS). This French word means "servant." It is a tradition at the Tour de France for the winner to give all his prize money to his teammates.

Lance, wearing the yellow jersey, is being shielded from the wind by his teammates.

shield: to protect
selfless: thinking of others before yourself

What Could Go Wrong?

By 1996, Lance had become a star.
He owned a big house on the banks of Lake
Austin, in Texas. He drove a sports car and
had won a great deal of money from his
races. He was ranked the number one cyclist
in the world. He had also just signed a
$2.5 million contract with a French cycling
team, Cofidis (KOH-fee-diss). It seemed
like Lance had it made.

But Lance was also tired. He developed
bronchitis (bron-KYE-tus) during the Tour
de France and quit the race early again.
Later, he was sixth in the Olympic Games
Individual Time Trial in Atlanta. It was an
event Lance should have won.

Despite not feeling well, Lance continued
to train and race. He believed he would
get better.

---

bronchitis: an illness of the throat and lungs that makes
you cough a lot

Cancer Strikes

On September 18, 1996, Lance had his 25th birthday. A few days later, he noticed that his right testicle was swollen. It was so sore that he couldn't ride his bike. He called his doctor at once. The doctor immediately sent Lance to see a specialist.

By early October, Lance had been diagnosed with testicular (tess-TI-kyu-lur) cancer. The cancer also had spread to his lungs. Lance couldn't believe it. He was young and strong. How could he have cancer?

Lance had been a fighter all his life. But could he fight cancer? What strengths might Lance have to help him battle this deadly disease?

---

testicle: a male reproductive organ that produces sperm
specialist: a doctor who is trained to treat a certain type of illness
diagnose: to recognize an illness by signs and symptoms

Chapter 3

Fight for Survival

Has your life ever changed suddenly? How did you react? Lance's life had been shattered by the news he had cancer. Suddenly, he was no longer fighting to be first at the finish line. He was fighting to stay alive!

Lance announces to reporters that he is being treated for cancer.

The First Week

The doctors had to act fast to stop Lance's cancer. They operated to remove his right testicle. After surgery, tests showed Lance was even sicker than they had thought. He had the most aggressive type of cancer. It had spread to his lungs, abdomen, and brain.

Lance's mother refused to give in. "This isn't going to get us," she said. Lance and his mom vowed that they would fight the disease—and win.

Lance started a drug treatment called chemotherapy (KEE-moh-thair-ah-pee). The chemotherapy drugs destroy cancer cells in the body. If this treatment worked, Lance would survive. But the drugs would damage Lance's lungs forever. Cyclists need healthy, strong lungs to race. Doctors said Lance would never race bikes again.

---

surgery: treatment of a disease or injury by cutting into and repairing or removing parts of the body
aggressive: active; spreading quickly
abdomen: the part of the body between the chest and hips
cell: a basic, microscopic part of an animal or a plant

Cancer

When someone has cancer, it means that some cells in his or her body are growing too fast. The cells can form lumps of tissue, called tumors. These tumors grow and infect body organs, often causing death.

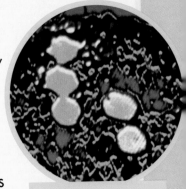

Untreated cancer cells can spread very fast.

Treatment

In chemotherapy treatment, the patient is given very strong drugs to kill the cancer cells in the body. Unfortunately, these drugs also kill healthy cells. This is why the patient becomes weak. Chemotherapy often has other bad side effects, such as nausea (NAW-zee-ah) and hair loss.

---

tissue: material that forms some part of a plant or animal
organ: a part of the body that does a particular job
nausea: feeling sick

A New Approach

An oncologist (on-CAH-lah-jist)—and cycling fan—named Dr. Steven Wolff called Lance. Wolff wanted Lance to try a different treatment. He told Lance that he should go to the Indiana University (IU) Medical Center in Indianapolis. This center treated cancer in a different way than Lance's doctors had prescribed.

Wolff believed that Lance could race again. It was important, said Wolff, that Lance get the right chemotherapy. Wolff hoped the doctors at the IU center could treat Lance's cancer without damaging his lungs.

First, the IU doctors would remove the lesions on Lance's brain. Then they would put him on chemotherapy. Like Wolff, these doctors believed Lance could win his cancer battle and race bikes again. They gave Lance hope.

---

oncologist: a doctor who treats cancer
prescribe: to give orders for medications or other treatments
lesion: an abnormal change in the body due to injury or illness

Support Network

Fast cars and big houses didn't matter to Lance anymore. He might never race again. In fact, he could die. Lance was scared. He needed his friends around him.

Lance had made many good friends in his life. Among them were Jim Ochowicz and Chris Carmichael. Both waited at the hospital for Lance to wake up after his brain surgery. But, of course, the first person Lance asked for was his mom.

Linda Armstrong was very important to Lance during the days and weeks that followed. She made charts of his chemotherapy treatments. She and Lance read all the books on cancer they could find. It was as if she and Lance were training for an important race. In a way, they were.

Lance Armstrong while undergoing chemotherapy
treatments for cancer

Coping with Chemotherapy

The brain surgery had worked. But Lance's chemotherapy treatment was now critical. The drugs were extremely powerful. If the cancer tumors did not get smaller after a couple of treatments, Lance would soon die.

The early tests were good, however. The cancer had stopped spreading. Blood tests showed that Lance's health was improving. He still had a long way to go, but this was a huge first step!

LaTrice Haney was one of the nurses who treated Lance. Haney administered the drugs and recorded his progress. She and Lance became good friends. They became "comrades in chemo," said Lance.

---

critical: very important
administer: to give
comrade: a friend or companion

But Lance was a difficult patient. He was in a hurry to get better. As his muscles grew weaker, he lost confidence. He began to think he would never be strong enough to compete again. Haney kept him focused, though. She told him that she wanted to see him on TV again one day, winning bike races.

Lance is shown here at home in Austin, Texas, during his recovery from cancer treatment.

---

focus: to fix your attention on something

More Problems

In late 1996, two weeks before Lance was diagnosed with cancer, he had signed a $2.5 million contract to race two years for Cofidis. After learning of Lance's disease, Cofidis agreed to pay him through 1997, even though he could not race.

Two months later, a member of the Cofidis team visited Lance in the hospital. He told Lance that Cofidis wanted to change Lance's contract. Cofidis didn't want to pay Lance's full salary, since he was not yet healthy enough to race. The contract said Lance had to take a medical exam. Cofidis asked Lance to take it. With cancer, Lance could not hope to pass it. He refused.

Finally, Cofidis and Lance reached an agreement. Lance had to ride in four races in 1997, or Cofidis could cancel his contract. "It felt like they thought I was dying," Lance said later.

Race against Cancer

But Lance did not intend to die. He compared his treatment to riding a time trial in the Tour de France. The time trial is a race against a stopwatch. This was a race against cancer. The doctors were his teammates, helping him compete. And guess what? Lance was winning.

Another Victory for Lance

On December 13, 1996, Lance had his final chemotherapy treatment. Tests now showed that the cancer was gone. But it could return at any time. If cancer did return, it most likely would appear in the next few months. All Lance could do was wait. Would he ever live a normal, healthy life again? Would he ever race again? Right now, there were more questions than answers.

— CHAPTER **4** —

A New Stage

Lance's treatment had worked, but his body was weak. Lance was also scared. What if the cancer came back? How could he live with that fear? Could a fear like that change your life? How?

Lance visits the Tour de France in July 1997 as he is recovering from cancer.

Riding for Pleasure

During treatment, Lance continued to ride his bike. His doctor warned that exercise would make him weaker. But Lance wanted to show people he was strong.

During one ride, an older woman pedaled past Lance on her mountain bike. She was not even out of breath! Lance was gasping for air.

Lance's rides got shorter and slower. On some days, he couldn't even make it around the block. Lance was putting too much pressure on himself. Lance needed to relax.

Lance finally decided it was time to ride for pleasure. He began to enjoy the fresh air and the freedom he felt on his bike. He enjoyed the wind on his face. He enjoyed just being alive.

Obligation of the Cured

While Lance was in the hospital, he met children who had cancer. He saw how scared they were. Lance's doctor told him about "the obligation of the cured."

Lance learned that he could help other cancer patients. He could comfort and encourage them. Lance had fought cancer and won. Now he could inspire others to do the same. More than 9 million Americans live with cancer. Lance realized he was part of that huge group. He wanted to help.

So he began the Lance Armstrong Foundation (LAF) to raise money for cancer research. The LAF planned a charity bike ride in Lance's hometown of Austin, Texas. It was called *Ride for the Roses*. The first ride, in March 1997, raised more than $200,000!

---

obligation: a promise or feeling of duty
encourage: to give someone hope or make someone feel more confident

Lance leads cyclists through the countryside during the Ride for the Roses bike ride, 2001.

Learning to Live

For Lance, there were still hard times ahead.
Chemotherapy had battered his body.
He was weak and could become ill easily.

Lance was tested every month. If the
cancer was coming back, it would be soon.
Lance hated those tests. "At least in chemo,
I was doing something," he said, "instead
of just waiting for it to come back."

He started riding again. Only a month
after leaving the hospital, he flew to France
to train with his team. Lance was still
always tired, though. Finally, doctors told
him to rest for the year. Training and racing
were out of the question.

Taking a Break

Lance decided to travel to Europe with his new girlfriend, Kristin "Kik" Richard. They had met during the Ride for the Roses. She was pretty, smart, and very independent. Lance fell in love with her.

Lance now saw Europe in a different way. He was no longer a racing cyclist, speeding through towns at 40 miles (64 kilometers) per hour. He was a tourist. For the first time, Lance wasn't training or competing. He was simply enjoying life.

Lance with Kristin Richard

Getting Back in Shape

On October 2, 1997, it had been one year since Lance learned he had cancer. The treatment had worked. Lance's cancer had not returned. His doctor sent him a note that said, "It's time to move on with your life."

Lance decided to do just that. He started training again. Lance spent two months at a training camp in California. He worked hard to get himself back in shape.

Even so, pro teams had little interest in Lance. They thought his career was over. Cofidis and Lance also could not agree on a contract for 1998. Lance's racing future didn't look very bright.

Linda Armstrong was able to raise her son's sinking spirits. She was always positive during the tough times for Lance. "They've made a terrible mistake," she said. "You'll show them."

Finally, an Offer

In late 1997, Lance finally received an offer to race. A new American team, the U.S. Postal Service Team, wanted to give Lance a chance. His salary would be about $200,000. It was less than half what a top rider could make. Lance would have to prove he could still ride like a champion.

On October 16, 1997, Lance tells reporters he will ride for the U.S. Postal Service Team.

End of the Road?

Lance moved to Europe for the start of the 1998 season. People were curious how he would do. The attention bothered him. Lance wanted more time to get used to racing again.

He finished 14th in his first event in Spain. Not bad for a cancer survivor! But Lance was unhappy. He was used to winning.

The next event was a stage race in France. The weather was awful. The rain lashed the riders. The temperature was freezing. Lance wondered why he was riding at all. He wanted to live a normal life.

Suddenly, Lance pulled over to the side of the road. He had had enough. He thought, *This is not how I want to spend my life....*

For the first time, Lance didn't want to race bikes anymore.

---

survivor: a person who recovers from an illness or accident
lash: to strike with force like a whip

Lance is back on his bike in 1998, but his comeback does not last long.

Champion of the Couch

Lance's friends were surprised. It was not like him to give up. But Lance was sure of his decision. He went home to Texas. He played golf. He sat around and watched TV. Lance wanted to be lazy.

Kik knew that Lance was confused. He was not the sort of person who sat around doing nothing. "I love you," she told him, "but you need to figure something out." Lance needed to decide what he was going to do with his life.

Finally, friends persuaded Lance to ride one more time—at his Ride for the Roses. It would be a farewell appearance for his fans.

But Lance wasn't in shape to race. He needed to get off the couch, out of the house, and back on his bike!

---

persuade: to encourage someone into action

Training Once Again

Chris Carmichael took Lance to North Carolina to train. Lance worked hard. He rode in the mountains every day for 10 days. He also began to enjoy riding his bike again.

One training ride included a long climb called Beech Mountain. Lance had been riding for nearly six hours. As he climbed, Lance started thinking about his life. He had a special talent. How could he waste it?

By the end of training camp, Lance had changed. "I got my life back on those rides," he said later. He decided to go back to Europe and race. He was never going to quit again.

But could Lance once again become a top-ranked professional cyclist? Or had cancer taken too much out of him? Only time—and a return to the Tour de France—would tell.

---

top-ranked: one of the best in a sport

CHAPTER 5

Against All Odds

Lance had beaten cancer and was back on his bike. He was determined to show the world he was still a champion. But how? There was only one way. He must try and win the Tour de France!

Lance rides in the Vuelta a España in September 1998.

Lance Rides Again

Lance returned to cycling in 1998 for the second time with renewed energy. Lance finished fourth in the U.S. Professional Championships. He and Kik, newly married, went back to France again in June 1998.

In September, Lance rode the Vuelta a España (VWEL-tah ah ess-SPAHN-yuh). The Vuelta is a tough, three-week stage race like the Tour de France.

Lance finished fourth overall and nearly won the hardest mountain stage. This was the best Lance had ever done in a three-week major tour. His rivals were surprised. He had never been a good mountain rider before. What had changed him?

The Vuelta proved that Lance was back and even better than before. He now believed that with a little more work, he could win the Tour de France.

A New Man

Cancer had changed Lance, in many ways. His body was nearly 20 pounds (9 kilograms) lighter. His attitude had also changed. He was a less aggressive rider. He was calm and focused.

Lance's director on the U.S. Postal Team wrote to him, "You will look great on the podium of the Tour de France next year." Lance wondered if it was true. Could he win the world's biggest bike race after all?

Route of the 1999 Tour de France

---

attitude: a way of acting or behaving that shows what a person is thinking or feeling
podium: a platform on which winners stand and receive their prizes

The Tour de France

"Le Tour," as the Tour de France is called, is the world's most important bike race. It lasts for three weeks and covers more than 2,000 miles (3,200 kilometers). The route changes every year, but it always includes at least six days in the Alps and the Pyrenees (peer-ah-NEEZ) mountains. This is the hardest part of the race.

The leader at the end of each day wears the famous "yellow jersey." Wearing the jersey for just one day is a huge feat. Wearing it at the finish of the race is the greatest prize in cycling.

Lance changes into the yellow jersey as the leader during the 1999 Tour de France.

Training for the Tour

In 1999, Lance made winning the Tour de France his goal. He skipped some early season races. He only rode in races that would help him prepare for the Tour in July. When he wasn't racing, Lance was training in the French mountains—the Alps or the Pyrenees.

His daily routine was punishing. There were more than 30 steep climbs near Lance's house in Nice (NEESE), France. Lance and his teammates trained on them all. Rides of seven hours each day were common.

There was one climb that Lance used to measure his fitness. Tony Rominger, a top Swiss rider, had ridden this steep, 8-mile (12.9-kilometer) slope in 31 minutes. In July, Lance rode it nearly a minute faster. He knew now that he was ready!

---

punishing: very physically difficult; harsh

Finally, the Race

Lance started the 1999 Tour de France in the best possible way. He won the opening time trial and wore the yellow jersey. The French call the time trial "the race of truth," because you must race alone against the clock without the help of your teammates. There were three time trial stages in 1999. Lance won them all.

Lance was slower in Stage 2, however, and gave up the yellow jersey. But he regained the yellow jersey after Stage 8. He was the overall leader again. Still, his rivals believed Lance would fall behind in the mountains. Even before cancer, he was no climber.

In fact, however, Lance was stronger than ever. He even won the first mountain stage in the Alps. By the finish in Paris, Lance had won the Tour de France by nearly eight minutes!

Celebration

At the finish of his first Tour de France championship, Lance celebrated with Kik, his mom, and his team. Back in Indiana, LaTrice Haney and the Indiana University medical staff watched on TV. "He did it," said Haney. "He conquered it."

Six in a Row

Lance's 1999 victory was the start of an amazing winning streak. Lance went on to win the Tour de France the next five years in a row, taking first in 2000, 2001, 2002, 2003, and 2004. No other rider had ever won the world's biggest cycling race six times. Lance had become the best Tour de France rider—ever.

Lance (left) rides with cancer survivors in the Tour of Hope, a cross-country ride to raise awareness and money for cancer research.

The Hope Machine

In 2001, the Lance Armstrong Foundation raised $16.1 million for cancer research and patient care programs. Lance was also appointed to the President's Cancer Panel.

When *Sports Illustrated* named Lance its 2002 Sportsman of the Year, the magazine said Lance was "...more than an athlete. He's become a kind of hope machine."

Lance says that he is a cancer survivor first and a cyclist second. But his biking success gives cancer patients everywhere hope and courage. This is what drives him on. "I just understand what they're going through," Lance says.

Epilogue

Time Line of Events
for Lance Armstrong

1991

- 1st, U.S. National Amateur Road Race Championship (USA)
- 1st, Settimana Bergamasca (Italy)

1992

- 1st, Thrift Drug Classic (USA)
- Signs professional contract with Motorola
- 2nd, Championship of Zurich (Switzerland)
- Member of the U.S. Olympic Team (Barcelona)

1993

- 1st, Thrift Drug Triple Crown (USA)
- Stage victory, Tour de France (France)
- 1st, U.S. Professional National Road Race Championship (USA)
- 1st, Professional World Road Race Championship (Norway)

1994

- 2nd, Liège-Bastogne-Liège (Belgium)
- 1st, Thrift Drug Classic (USA)

1995

- 1st, Tour du Pont (USA)
- Stage victory, Tour de France (France)
- 1st, Classica San Sebastián (Spain)

1996

- 1st, Tour du Pont (USA)
- 1st, Flèche Wallone (Belgium)
- 2nd, Liège-Bastogne-Liège (Belgium)
- Member of the U.S. Olympic Team (Atlanta)
- Diagnosed with testicular cancer

1997

- Founds Lance Armstrong Foundation
- Declared cancer-free
- Signs contract with U.S. Postal Service Team

1998

- 1st, Tour of Luxembourg (Luxembourg)
- Marries Kristin (Kik) Richard

1999

- 1st, Tour de France (France)—4 stage wins
- Son Luke David born

2000

- 1st, Tour de France (France)—1 stage win
- 1st, Grand Prix Eddy Merckx (Belgium)
- 1st, Grand Prix des Nations (France)
- Member of the U.S. Olympic Team (Sydney)

2001

- 1st, Tour of Switzerland (Switzerland)
- 1st, Tour de France (France)—3 stage wins
- Twin daughters Isabelle Rose and Grace Elizabeth born

2002

- 1st, Midi Libre (France)
- 1st, Dauphine Libère (France)
- 1st, Tour de France (France)—4 stage wins